It *Was* Rigged..!

...Just Not How You Think

by

Younger Kaufman, MBA

A little history

You may recall one of the more famous verbal stumbles to draw criticism was the use of the word "covfefe" shortly after Charlottesville became a national focus as a hotbed of racial tension. Rather than clarify himself, Donald Trump left the meaning of his word ambiguous. This delay and hope it goes away tactic is one he regularly employs.

Unfortunately, he missed a rare opportunity to unite the country in a time when the national conversation was shifting further toward discord.

Suppose the concept he sought to express was that of La Convivencia. Suppose he has discussed Kabbalah with Jared and Ivanka and learned about the time that produced Maimonides. It is thought that in southern Spain around the turn of the first millennium that Christians, Jews, and Muslims all lived together in harmony.[i]

How tenuous the peace actually was is debatable. It was a time of great scientific, artistic, and cultural development. Using this concept would have been an elegant response to the situation. The example could have led to our focusing on the common interests that unite us and perhaps some community building.

We all flub a word from time to time; a little clarification would have gone a long way to achieving his intended purposes. Instead he let a bruised ego dictate he continue down the path for which he was already taking heat. He went back to his base for an ego boost and spewed more of the vitriol he could so easily have overcome. He maintains his claim the word meant more.[ii] If it did have some deeper meaning, then he deliberately cowered so as not to look soft. To maintain the support of a few, he did not earn the respect of many.

This brings us to our first lesson:

Own it.

Have conviction while facing adversity. Don't stop until you get your idea across. Deal with the situation at hand while maintaining your beliefs and values despite any fear of what others may say. In the end if you're wrong, it may just wash. If you're right, who knows? You just might change the world.

It must have been humiliating being the trust fund college kid being laughed at by the regular workers as he pushed a broom through the first real-estate project Donald Trump tried to take credit for. He would tell his peers at UPenn (reports sketchy as to existence of actual friends) that the apartment complex deal his father was flipping had his name all over it. That name being: "The Cincinnati Kid"[iii] The brand began with Donald lying to try and gain respect without earning it. From these shaky foundations would rise the entire house of cards. The psychology of the man now running the free world was shaped by the isolation and anger that comes with being a habitual liar who is bad at lying. When one stands true to oneself, respect is earned. The one thing Donny wants most and can't figure out.

The example illustrates the second lesson:

Earn it.

What initially shapes one's brand is under one's control. From the conception of the idea one wants to convey, self awareness is key. What ultimately shapes a brand will be the mind of the consumer; because of this the message sent must be cohesive throughout.

He has had success, but for a brand to last there needs to be some substance in the character of the person or persons behind it. At one time, Trump Enterprises was in the real estate business. There were tangible assets represented on its financial statements. However, the man was out of his league in the New York real estate scene and quickly ran into hundreds of millions of dollars in debt. While the actual players were doing quite well, he was declaring bankruptcy to avoid paying contractors and investors.[iv] Who knows what happened to the money he borrowed to do as much? The deals he has made over the years since have made profits for him and not many others involved. This is because he just licenses his name. Most of the actual properties take losses while he benefits.[v]

This is the core of the concern. The business practices being applied to this administration aren't focused on the concerns of the people. We began with talking the talk, this is the walking the walk aspect of business and life. Take credit only for what you yourself accomplish. Don't say one thing and do the other. If you're going to support the military, then insulting veterans and gold-star families will damage your brand.[vi] At least it should.

We seem to be getting ahead of ourselves and into the election. Let's examine the campaign and the applied marketing concepts that ultimately led to its success. Let's get down to business.

It Was Rigged

Remember branding is ultimately in the mind of consumers.[vii] Marketing is how companies influence it. But, not how you think. If you've never had a business class, then when you hear the word "marketing" the concept that comes to mind is probably actually advertising.

So far, we've discussed a certain mindset needed for success in business and life - basically, being a person of integrity. Sure, you can cheat and get ahead, but at what cost?

We are going to view the campaign as if it were its own company within the Trump Enterprise. A business plan would be their plan of attack. Any business plan needs an exit strategy – going public, selling it outright or just being a going concern or investment. The exit strategy in this case was winning the election to the presidency. In that regard the company was a success. It continues to be a going concern, except now he might get the public to pay for his trips to hold rallies.[viii] Writing off that kind of expense would be a boon for any business. It's just one benefit of the world of politics.

A large component of any good business plan is a marketing plan. The reason being – that is where the work happens. Marketing is the engine that turns an idea into an actuality, the figurative to the literal. So what the hell is marketing anyway?

Look up marketing wherever you look stuff up and you will find it is basically the implementation of the marketing mix, otherwise known as the four p's - product, price, place, and promotion.[ix] The mix pretty much encompasses the whole business effort. Beautiful women selling you beer is only a small piece of the puzzle. But since that is what comes to mind why not start there?

Promotion

There can be no doubt; the rally was the tool used to win. From hiring people to watch him descend the escalator to his hectic finale run during the last few days of the campaign, Trump used the crowd to create an illusion of popularity.[x] This is where the man shines. He exploits thinking errors. He kept himself in the daily news cycle by constantly saying the next controversial thing to his followers. After so many outlandish statements, most of the public was overwhelmed and became numb to the hate he was spreading, but not his followers.

The news media was caught unprepared. They didn't know how to deal with him, and he was generating ratings after all. The polls and pundits had him as a long shot and the networks had a lot of time to fill. This is where the rigging happens. Trump owes CNN a huge thank you, the most effective aspect of the whole campaign was the opportunity for his surrogates to spin stories however they liked and then talk over almost all responses.[xi] Revisit current press secretary Kayleigh McEnany's performance as a surrogate. They were able to exploit the media's methods to control the message, and they had to cover-up for some substantive issues. Remember the 17 women who have accused him of sexual harassment?[xii] Remember him bragging about sexually assaulting women?[xiii]

It was Kellyanne Conway's job to get you to forget those facts and focus on the underdog that the media was treating unfairly. Her poisoning the well tactics were another thinking error used to confuse valid concerns in the coverage of her boss.[xiv] They portrayed the media as the enemy to discredit the validity of the daily negative stories as well as shift attention away from the actual issues involving the candidate.

Advertising is almost an afterthought. Attack ads are, unfortunately, a staple of politics. If you're going to watch TV or stream something for free, then you're going to see them every couple years or so. There is a lot of money poured into the industry, most of which comes from super-PACs.[xv] It is worth mentioning there were borderline violations, but I digress.[xvi] We were talking about rigging.

There is a lesson to be learned in there about planning and implementation. I will give them credit; they executed their public relations strategy skillfully. Honestly, in business there is a fine line we walk. We can use people's thinking errors to persuade them, but we need to have a foundation in ethics. Scott Adams, the "dilbert" cartoonist, has remarked several times that his friend Donald tries to use hypnosis.[xvii] You know how he repeats things several times? Thousands of years ago a philosopher used his idea of the enthymeme to illustrate persuasion in its most potent form.[xviii] The idea being that one convinces the other it was their idea to begin with.

So what is it they were trying so hard to sell you?

Product

Typically, you think of a product as something tangible like a car or a golf club. In associating the realness of something with a product you might think Trump himself is the product he is selling. This is wherein the trick lies. It's hot air in a gaslight; a shadow of a ghost is all that is produced. The image of what this man would be able to do as President was easily malleable.

As a businessman he should have had the acumen to oversee such a vast organization. Trump says he took a "small" million-dollar loan from his father and turned it into an empire worth billions. That's what he claims anyway.[xix]

As a negotiator he should have had the intelligence to understand complex international agreements, and the conviction to stand firm for the interests of Americans. After entering three of the past four election cycles, he should have had some concept these were things the people wanted.[xx]

The idea of Trump for president seemed laughable.[xxi] But when he entered a field of 15 primary candidates, statistics did the rigging for him. When it came to politics, only three of five people voted.[xxii] The average voter barely knew the candidates' names. As mentioned earlier the brand Trump had been steadily creeping into the American psyche for nearly forty years with a recent decade long boost thanks to his reality show. Name recognition gave him an edge that he sharpened by constantly gaming the news cycle.[xxiii] Getting his name out there is one thing the man definitely knows.

The same name that ran up a billion dollars in debt for his "successful" business is what was pitched.[xxiv] A champion of everything, a workingman's hero to "drain the swamp" and "shake things up" was on his way to Washington.

The conservative agenda was part of the package. Hundreds of judgeships and perhaps even a few on the Supreme Court were at stake. Tax cuts and scrapping Obamacare were promised as easy legislation. Christian values would be American values, dammit.[xxv]

This idea of a tough business guy turned world leader was enough for most. For some there was an option for a bonus, a sense of community bounded by the notion that their rights transcended those of others whom they considered unworthy.

Place

They say the embarrassment showing on Trump's face during the first news conference was due to the exposition of his want to be a Russian spy. He is not the type to be bashful about the other thing.

I don't know, but they say Trump and associates made deals with some of his fellow republican candidates in order to get them in the race in the first place. Diluting the pool would increase his odds. Interesting conspiracy theory and obviously I have no proof of such an assertion, so why even make

the claim? Only to illustrate Trump's favorite tool -
the lie.

Take a course in forensics and the very first day one
learns it is nothing like CSI. In forensics, or
argumentation, one learns to present a sound
argument with evidence to support it. One also
learns about fallacies, concepts like straw man,
slippery slope or ad hominem among others. These
are thinking errors in psychology and at the very
least are not valid as evidence for a claim.[xxvi]

So, what does this have anything to do with a
discussion about place in marketing?

Well, it used to be that one would walk into a brick
and mortar store to buy one's batteries, sneakers, or
vehicle. The actual place was the final point of
contact to get the message across before the sale.
These days, place has become ethereal. Between
the internet and cable there is not much information
one does not have access to. Manipulating the
message has become increasingly complex and
diffuse yet easier to deliver as the consumer is

making purchases from their bathroom. Place is now wherever the message is delivered. It extends from living rooms and movie theaters to board rooms and vacation days.

To quote the Beastie Boys, "I said, 'Where'd you get your information from,' huh?"[xxvii]

Message is the meaning, or concept, one wants to convey through a medium to another. Noise is any interference that distorts that meaning.[xxviii] It is not limited to being between the source and the audience; it can occur both before and after the message is either delivered or received. Confused yet? That's the point.

When the man can make any claim he wants and attribute it to "they" and move on to the next lie before the correct information surfaces, then the noise generated begins to generate a resonance that overwhelms the end consumer - the voter. Evidence can be seen in the tapes of surrogates Corey Lewandowski, Kellyanne Conway, or others literally talking over other pundits to make noise and muddle the message. This strategy should only work in a blitz when the consumer is rushed to decide without all the relevant information. This could have been borrowed from a hard sale at a used car lot. Just as there are still brick-and-mortar stores, there were actual places where this sale took place. Sure, it stared with a few paid observers in the lobby of Trump Tower. It grew though to scores of people cheering and chanting and even a few assaulting dissenters and members of the media nightly in cities across the country and continues still.[xxix]

The lies had to originate somewhere. In the two decades he had been running for president and his decade as a reality show figure he gained one crucial insight into the information industry. Money drives it. What Trump needed was attention, so he took the show on the road.

The public relations strategy Trump employed saved him millions. Sure, he was using his own money to run, but travel is not the real expense of a campaign.[xxx] Getting your name into American homes is.

News media executives saw advertising dollars in the coverage and perhaps thought, "What's the harm?" None of their polls had Trump for the win and twenty-four hours is a lot of time to fill in a day. The media gave him just about all the free advertising he wanted. The more outlandish the claims he made, the more he was reported on, and the more like-minded individuals came out to support him.

This created an illusion. In forensics it is called an appeal to popularity.

The candidate made sure to emphasize the media wasn't reporting on the crowd sizes, shouting about how he wasn't getting a fair shake.[xxxi] This set up the devil's best trick - convincing you that he is you.

You- guy on the couch not getting a fair shake and mad at the politicians that promised you one. You- gal whose job went somewhere else. Don't look at my overseas manufacturing; look at how they're all mean to me just like they're mean to you.

They're called fallacies for a reason. They are used in lieu of evidence to try to cheat reason. Rather than say how he's going to get you a job, he's going to place your blame on "them." He's going to try and convince you that place takes place inside your mind. It's only kind of creepy, but definitely tightens the rigging.

The people that turned out to the rallies were more a part of the marketing package than they were the end consumer. But the target market they represented were a stubborn and noisy bunch, ideal for his political ends. Remember, place reaches to the last opportunity to get a message across. Remember voter suppression and intimidation tactics?[xxxii] The former was a benefit of securing the republican nomination; the latter was specific to Trump's campaign.

Price

Once candidate Trump became the Republican nominee by playing the numbers' game, the cost of the campaign shifted. This placed him in the familiar position of benefiting from someone else footing the bill. Cost is ultimately what determines price. A business will not stay in business very long by selling something for less than it takes to make it. It also cannot sell something for more than the buyer determines its inherent value to be. Remember, the product they were selling was a presidency.
What then was the price?
It would appear to be the average citizen's vote. That is a complicated currency, though. For those loyal to the party there may be actual money or time contributions helping fund the party and the campaign. This is a small portion, but it represents most partisan voters. The average voter will typically vote along party lines regardless of the candidate,

and better than 90 percent did so in the last election.[xxxiii]

There are more than a few "us vs. them mentality" studies that delve into the psychology of the phenomena.[xxxiv] It is interesting to note these concepts are currently being researched by the highest levels of our national security.[xxxv]

Suffice it to say brand loyalty is only one point where business and politics intersect. Partisan voters then pay twice. They are giving their support on the back end and their vote on the front. The party itself had to adjust its values and acceptable tolerance of indignities.

The real price has yet to be determined. Our system being of the people and for the people means the average citizen will have to bear the brunt of a tax giveaway to the ultra-wealthy, environmental harm from deregulation, and ever increasing health costs and service cuts.

The campaign made the next lesson obvious:

Create it.

Kellyanne did her research and knew how to manipulate the electoral system to pull off the seemingly impossible. Due diligence is the work you put into learning about the investment and creating a plan to reach the optimal result. They were successful because they created a base designed specifically for the purpose of their product being sold. They made their own market from conceptualization through implementation and rode it into the administration.

An appeal to popularity and other common thinking errors helped the team control and spin the message and narratives. Misdirection was expertly used to get an image of a president elected without giving away too much truth about the little man cowering behind the curtains. The trouble is that slight of hand left us woefully unprepared for the lack of substance necessary to lead the executive branch of our government.

Just Not How You Think

Forget all the bleeding-heart stuff just discussed with marketing and let's get mean as we examine management with the administration. Business is not nice. It is cold, hard and driven by tangible influences. That doesn't mean in order to be successful a business can't make deals that benefit all involved.[xxxvi] It means we are only concerned about their benefit so long as we profit from it.
A business is a going concern. Specifically, this means while it is solvent it has a fiduciary duty to its stakeholders and nothing more.[xxxvii] This is the core of capitalism - the field on which the game is played.

Russia was deliberately left out of the election discussion because the public only had bits of information and suspicions at the time. Now we know there was plenty of collusion at attempts to cover it, bordering on criminal actions. Only the ineptness of the actors prolonged the drama until impeachment was introduced due to attempts to blatantly offer a sovereign nation a quid-pro-quo for baseless information on a possible political opponent.[xxxviii]

Management begins from the top. The character of the person or persons leading the organization will impact its benefit to stakeholders. Ultimately, the idea is to optimize the exploitation of resources to maximize said benefit. We want to continue this into perpetuity, and this is where character comes into play. Are you going to buy something from someone you do not trust? That's marketing and an external relationship, but it's the fulcrum in the process. Relationships are a key aspect of management. When you think of your boss, do you think of them as the person that hired you and their job is dealing with you and your coworkers? Even though this is only one aspect of management we are conditioned to think it stops there.

"I'll hire only the best people," is an outstanding strategy if you plan to actually utilize their knowledge, skills, and abilities. Organizational behavior and human resources are essential components of our process to exploit raw material for benefit. We need people in order to accomplish every step, whether it's the person who designed the machine or the one feeding metal into it; the miners whom pulled the ore from the ground or the mine owners minding their finances. These internal relationships change that metal into coin.

To balance this section with the last, we will examine Koontz and O'Donnell's five functions of management as it pertains to the administration.[xxxix] These serve as an excellent framework for what an organization wants to accomplish. We could go back to Fayol and the principles but suffice it to say that management is a dynamic ongoing process. We can learn as much from bad examples as from good. Considering the subject...

Planning

Setting goals is the first step. Where one wants to go determines the direction taken to get there. Short-term goals provide a catalyst. Tasks are established; how they will be accomplished and by whom will be the busy aspect of the business. Utilizing resources optimally is what a company hopes to achieve. Long-term strategy combines these efforts to produce a whole greater than the sum of its parts. This creates the vision a company has, which remains largely unchanged though planning in itself is a fluid process.

The administration began with plans including the border wall, killing the Affordable Care Act (Obamacare), tax restructuring, and some vague foreign relations and trade intentions.
As of writing this, just months from the election, only three miles of new barrier have been constructed along the border.[xl] This issue Trump seemed to care

so deeply about would be a perfect stage for him to demonstrate his management prowess. As a negotiating tactic he shut down the government, only to cave on his demands and accept a fraction of the previous offer.[xli]

He couldn't manage to get Obamacare repealed in congress because they couldn't figure out how to replace it. Certain members of congress felt it unethical to leave constituents without health care. President Trump turned to a tool he had criticized President Obama for using, the executive action. His first order of business in office was to issue a worthless one saying he'd do something about Obamacare.[xlii] He's currently considering another executive action to cover pre-existing conditions. Obamacare did this already.[xliii]

Mitch McConnell and Paul Ryan managed the tax bill and almost put $800 into the average American family's pocket.[xliv] Trump then introduced sanctions to China, and took $2,300 out of the average American family's pocket.[xlv]

He offered to negotiate with Indo-Pacific countries bilaterally with no new takers.[xlvi] His perceived instability may have contributed to players in the region spending more on defense, though.[xlvii] He made a $100 billion dollar deal with Saudi Arabia of which only money from Obama administration deals has come through.[xlviii] He then tried to sneak $8 billion past congress through an emergency declaration.[xlix] He did stand up for their leader when some convincing evidence implicated the young man in directing the gruesome murder of a journalist.[l] There was talk of some secret deal to let Russia handle America's cyber security.[li] There was a bomb drop and a missile attack and it all seems a little scattershot.[lii] [liii]

All these tasks were carried out by some very accomplished individuals, but to what end? This is the reason why planning is so essential. The ideal is a cohesive vision that planning enables.

Organizing

Do you know how an internal combustion engine works? Changing old dinosaurs into open road exhilaration takes a lot of moving parts each doing their part. It takes metal to build it and fuel to run it. An engine company could acquire or establish its source material itself in order to keep costs down. Vertical integration is how Ford did it, and how Carnegie brought steel to industry. A refining company could buy its competition and use horizontal integration to build a fortune like Rockefeller.[liv] These open to economies of scale and scope and are examples of competitive advantages made possible by organizing these organizations to optimally utilize their assets and resources.[lv]

A president has the benefit of stepping into an already established hierarchical organization, albeit one of the most complicated ones ever created. People are in place to accomplish tasks utilizing available resources in order to keep America going. It can be overwhelming, let us just focus on one plan he had in the last section.

Examine the case of the border wall, congressional leadership offered the president the $25 billion he asked for the wall.[lvi] The master negotiator turned them down, shut down the government and then settled for less. Nonetheless, the means were there. Management is a fluid process, but for this project the organization was already in place. Government employees were ready to push papers to fund work done by companies built to bid on government contracts and improve the country's infrastructure. The money sat there. Trucks didn't roll. Cement didn't get poured. Hard working average Joes didn't collect paychecks on jobs they believed they had voted for.[lvii]

Optimally utilizing assets makes or breaks businesses. Having the right person in the right place at the right time with the right tools to do the job is the result of our planning. An organization is a system. Organization is utilizing systems to change our plans into results.

Staffing

In business theory, employees are an expense.[lviii] Their knowledge, skills and abilities make business happen, ultimately though, they are just another resource. That's why it's called human resources and this management function sometimes isn't addressed independently. In practice, people are complicated creatures and a deft touch is required for an organization to utilize them most effectively and efficiently.

Leadership is a key influence when it comes to staffing. Organizational behavior develops from the top down. The people the boss likes get ahead, and their ideas drive a businesses' direction. The boss may like them because they work hard and have good ideas – that is a sign of health.

A few examples stand out with this administration. Rex Tillerson stepped into the Secretary of State roll with a background as an oil company executive. His years of dealing in a globalized marketplace showed. He had a sensible approach to geopolitical issues and was making good decisions. Unfortunately, his boss undermined his efforts at nearly every turn. In relations with North Korea, for example, Tillerson laid the groundwork for some complex negotiations.[lix] Trump stepped in, wanting to play the hero, and instead got played.

Like a spoiled child Trump just wants attention. He wants people to do what he wants, when he wants, and how he wants like William Barr does.[lx] This is probably the reason he turned to the Federalist Society to provide him a list of Supreme Court Justice Nominations.[lxi]

Being the only one to make money in his business dealings for using his name, he has not learned how to deal with people. The man famous for saying "you're fired" cannot even do the same in real life.[lxii]

Case after case has shown this leadership has been more concerned with its image than the task at hand. Capable people were ousted for doing their job while those that supported Trump in seemingly corrupt actions were kept around.[lxiii] Again, having the best people for the job means letting them do their job and accepting wise council. Typical organizations cannot thrive without some differences of opinion. Whether a company treats its employees as robots or with the respect due an individual is entirely up to management. There are many studies and plenty of evidence in successful companies showing that more satisfied employees are typically more productive.

Satisfaction is a subjective concept. Some are motivated by money or career advancement and some by personal development. Organizations can accomplish great things, but they need capable people to do so. Staffing envelops all this to make a whole that is greater than the sum of its parts.

Directing

Leadership is a central tenant of management. This aspect of the directing function serves as catalyst for all organizations' ongoing efforts. Effective managers are not just there to supervise people; they're there to develop optimal performance with the workforce. Having the right person for the job is good but insufficient. That person needs to be properly motivated. This can be as simple as a well-timed compliment. There are situations that require more finesse, such as a pay raise or termination threat. Communication skills are essential - tact and couth are traits commonly found in effective managers.[lxiv]

"You're fired!"[lxv] It is ironic that this catchphrase defined this man for so many years. Despite publicly criticizing his subordinates in immature ways, he could not find the courage of conviction to say those words in person to any of the people he dismissed. Most of these were due to contradiction to or lack of support for Trump's many false narratives. He values loyalty more than ability.

Leaks and turnover have been the markers of this administration. Chiefs of staff have simply given up when overwhelmed by the chaos and confusion the president deliberately created. Press conferences were cancelled indefinitely. Apparently it became too difficult for even Sarah Sanders to keep track of all the untruths. It's easier for Trump to do his own gas-lighting; he's been practicing all his life. Trump brought the briefings back (with threats to cancel them again) only once coronavirus threatened the economy.[lxvi]

Leadership means having the backbone to stand by your principles. People recognize this and respect it. It lends credence to your character. A claim to value strength is strengthened by having values. Something as simple as a person's stance on vaping can show a great deal about that person.[lxvii] Something as complex as withdrawing troops to allow the ethnic cleansing of a group that has heavily contributed to your country's safety can show a great deal more.[lxviii]

Control

How is success measured? Surely, it is deeper than just financial statements. It is. And don't call you Shirley?[lxix] Financial statements are a representation of how healthy a business is at a certain point in time. If business is being conducted efficiently and effectively, the numbers should be evidence. They can vary by industry and the stage of life the business is in. There are many other markers an enterprise can use as basis for improvements. External factors can be influential, but our focus must remain on what we can do internally. Therefore, we have controls.[lxx]
To minimize risk, a business establishes plans and implements them as well as can be done with what information is available. Business is a dynamic endeavor. Mistakes are made to be learned from.

Standards are established and measurements are made against them to optimize a business' operations. Corrective measures need to be taken to better optimize resources in a dynamic environment. Successful processes are examined and used further to improve overall performance. The control function is continuous and applied to the entire enterprise.[lxxi]

There is a system of checks and balances written into our constitution which is roughly analogous to our examination of this administration as if it were a business. The measurements are to be applied to the administration's implementation of its plans. National security is an area where strict controls are needed. An attack on this republic was carried out in cyberspace by a sovereign state.[lxxii] After the first clandestine meeting with the leader of said state, the person most responsible for the nation's security talked of an agreement to turn over the government's cyber-security efforts to those responsible for the attack.[lxxiii] Congress had to force the administration to implement sanctions.[lxxiv] This actually happened.

While Trump rallied against the southern border, the majority of those on terrorist watch lists caught sneaking into this country on his watch came from the other direction.[lxxv]

With control there is a need for focus on the systems that are essential to an organization's overall purpose. Realistic approaches are the key. Trump was offered $25 billion to build his wall. He instead shut down the government and settled for less. Again, with only a few months remaining in his term, only a few miles have been built. A private company built some wall that he seemed to claim as proof, until it began crumbling a few months later. That company then won another $1.7 billion in contracts for more wall.[lxxvi] Seems an apt metaphor for why control is necessary.

Cause and Effect

It may surprise you, but the president should actually have little to do with the economy. That being said, there are a couple of ways a president can have a large impact on the economy. The executive branch managed to shut down a large part of the government. The economy was suppressed in one fail swoop. The reason given was that more money was needed for a wall with Mexico.[lxxvii] The government reopened after Trump signed a deal with tens of billion less in funding than was offered before the shutdown.[lxxviii] Hundreds of billions vanishing from the economy due to lost productivity may have forced his hand.

Coming from a real estate background, Donald Trump knows there is a great deal of money to be made in times of inflation.[lxxix] Personally, he did not do so well, but he saw people in the his line of business in New York during inflationary times take full advantage of those times.[lxxx]

Breaking long standing convention he used the office of the president to speak against the Federal Reserve Chairman's decisions to adjust the lending rate.[lxxxi] Time and again he criticized the Chairman.[lxxxii] He even tried to implant his former surrogate on the board.[lxxxiii]

His attempts to play the role of the "best" economist ever were laissez faire and somewhat harmless while the economy was still strong. An unprecedented challenge came roaring across the globe to silence all economies. A time when strong leadership and keen insight will alter the course of history is at hand and the "very stable genius" in the bully pulpit believes telling citizens that maybe injecting sanitizer will be enough to restore their confidence in going shopping.[lxxxiv]

Congress moved to approve trillions in spending, most of which was directed to corporations that, thanks to the recent tax cuts, no longer pay enough taxes to support the system being drained.

Meanwhile, small businesses suffer and even more goes out in stimulus to unemployed workers whose taxes are not going back in.[lxxxv]

Do you see the problem?

Let's again examine history. Natives in America traded shells, stones and beads as a representation of value. This is the basis of currency. A shared belief that that thing represented a certain portion of some tangible good is what allowed civilization to grow.

Move forward to European colonization and an agrarian economy, things get a little more complex. Introduce industrialization and things really kick into high gear. Let's slow down here and look at just where macroeconomics in the modern age begins.

Henry C Carey wrote the books establishing American economic theory.[lxxxvi] He served as chief economic advisor to President Lincoln. His early thought tended toward free trade but eventually he turned to a position of protectionism. This was the

1800's and meant government oversight of private enterprise, unlike today. It also meant tariffs and reduced trade among nations, a strategy the current administration has pursued since its conception. Again, this was the 1800's. The reasoning was that nutrients from the rich southern soil would be transferred to enrich England.

President Trump would seemingly like to go further and completely close the borders. He does not understand that for a nation to take an isolationist stance it must be self-sufficient. Japan before the Second World War is an example. How much of what you rely on comes from some other part of the world?

Tax cuts inhibited the government's ability to satisfy its obligations. Savings for corporations went to stock repurchases; their obligation is to the stakeholder. Unfortunately, the cuts needed a roughly 4% economic growth rate just to maintain the government's cash flow requirements.[lxxxvii] At the time it was half that. Any economic growth from the

cuts had been lost before the pandemic.[lxxxviii] Now…
Unemployment spiking dramatically has made some
growth possible, but the trillions of dollars spent in
stimulus have had to come from somewhere. These
are precarious times. Businessman Trump would
most likely like the government to just start printing
excess money and stop taking old notes out of
circulation. He would like to flood the economy with
currency and devalue that dollar in your pocket.
He wants inflation but is risking stagflation to gain it.
What does he care? He can get a wheelbarrow full
of dollars. Coupling an isolationist position with
deficit spending is a recipe for disaster – the fallout
from which we may be dealing with for some time to
come.

One only need look to the past. Most current
macroeconomic theory was begun shortly after the
Great Depression by a man named John Maynard
Keynes. Government intervention at the time was
used to stabilize the economy and save people from
the hardships they faced.

Keynes looked at the total spending in the economy; he called this aggregate demand. Because it behaves erratically, the production capacity of an economy is affected. Instability in spending (recession or inflation) influences production and employment. During times of inefficient outcomes intervention in monetary policy by the central bank and even fiscal policy measures on the government's part can be used as stabilizing tools. [lxxxix] The Obama administration utilized this thinking to leave Trump an economy on the rise.[xc]

Trump wanted to reverse any government oversight and corrective policy his predecessor had put in place simply for spite without consideration of consequences. He also unabashedly sought to influence fiscal policy for his own financial gains. Keynesian economics broke down when stagflation took hold during the oil crisis in the late 70's. They were unprecedented times with an outside variable acting as a heavy lever. There was resurgence in the thought after the housing bubble collapsed and the economy again had to recover. The country is not energy independent.[xci] It is vulnerable in many other areas, both literally and figuratively. Basically, a market economy reflects the psychology of those involved in it. Uncertainty leads to an increase in saving and reduction in consumption and investment. These are unprecedented times with an outside variable acting as a heavy lever.

As businesspeople we can exploit the current situation. That is what business is - exploiting resources and situations to our advantage. This does not mean screw over the next guy; it means take stock of what's available and make the most of it. There are opportunities anywhere you make them and they in turn will allow you to make opportunities for others. Businesses are moving toward ever more socially responsible positions. The influences that decide the strength of the economy may very well be tied to our response to the pandemic. Care for others, not just profits has become a welcome theme across industries. It is only a little ironic that market leaders are taking advantage of these shifts to sustain and even grow through these difficult times.

The days of the slick 80's sleazeball businessman stereotype are over. Trump will soon be irrelevant again.

The final lesson is:

The most important thing you can bring to the table is them.

Communication and collaboration are keys to success in whatever endeavor you chose to undertake. Be bold yet understanding with all whom you deal. I will leave you with a quote from *Atlas Shrugged*.

"Any man who's afraid of hiring the best ability he can find, is a cheat who's in business where he doesn't belong. To me-the foulest man on earth, more contemptible than a criminal, is the employer who rejects men for being too good. That's what I've always thought and-say what are you laughing at?"[xcii]

Afterword – Tan

The attorneys insist I address the marketing of this book. In promoting this book three things were offered. Here are the deliverables.

1 Tactics and strategies to use to save the election – If you're going to vote for Trump, STAY HOME! You obviously don't make good decisions.

2 Arguments to use against snowflakes – I have not met a group of people that complain as much as maga does. The thinnest skinned one is the leader. I'll give him what he's always wanted though, a tan so deep it won't wash off like that orange stuff. It's his name now – **Tan Trump**

3 Taking care of business – did ya learn somethin'?

References

[i] Carrol, James. Constantine's Sword: The Church and the Jews. Boston, Massachusetts: Houghton Mifflin Harcourt, 2002.

[ii] Gallucci, Nicole. "Trump's still arguing that 'covfefe' tweet had 'deep meaning' and is not 'a mistweet'" Mashable, 24 Nov 2019, https://mashable.com/article/donald-trump-covfefe-tweet-horse/

[iii] Mannepalli, Aswin. "Was Trump's First Deal Really So Successful?" Bisnow, 28 Oct 2016, https://www.bisnow.com/national/news/construction-development/trumps-first-deal-look-in-cincinnati-66977

[iv] Swanson, Ana. "The myth and the reality of Donald Trump's business empire" The Washington Post, 29 Feb 2016, https://www.washingtonpost.com/news/wonk/wp/2016/02/29/the-myth-and-the-reality-of-donald-trumps-business-empire/

[v] Olenski, Steve. "Donald Trump's Real Secret To Riches: Create A Brand And License It" Forbes, 24 Nov 2015, https://www.forbes.com/sites/steveolenski/2015/11/24/donald-trumps-real-secret-to-riches-create-a-brand-and-license-it/#7c77155e3622

[vi] Rodgers, Tom, et al. "Op-Ed: Gold Star Families 'Disgraced' by Trump at Helsinki Summit" Military.com, 23 Jul 2018, https://www.military.com/daily-news/2018/07/23/op-ed-gold-star-families-disgraced-trump-helsinki-summit.html

[vii] Berkowitz, Eric, et al. Marketing 6th Edition. New York City, New York: Irwin/McGraw-Hill, 2000.

[viii] Goldmacher, Shane, and Shorey, Rachel. "Trump's Tulsa Rally Drew Sparse Crowd, but It Cost $2.2 Million" The New York Times, 21 Jul 2020, https://www.nytimes.com/2020/07/21/us/politics/trump-tulsa-rally-cost.html

[ix] Needham, Dave. Business for Higher Awards. Oxford, England: Heinemann, 1996.

[x] Bump, Phillip. "Even the firm that hired actors to cheer Trump's campaign launch had to wait to be paid" The Washington Post, 20 Jan 2017, https://www.washingtonpost.com/news/the-fix/wp/2017/01/20/even-the-firm-that-hired-actors-to-cheer-trumps-campaign-launch-had-to-wait-to-be-paid

xi Loofbourow, Lili. "How Kellyanne Conway became the greatest spin doctor in modern American history" The Week, 31 Jan 2017, https://theweek.com/articles/675240/how-kellyanne-conway-became-greatest-spin-doctor-modern-american-history

xii Keneally, Meghan. "List of Trump's accusers and their allegations of sexual misconduct: The president has repeatedly denied all the accusations." abcnews, 25 Jun 2019, https://abcnews.go.com/Politics/list-trumps-accusers-allegations-sexual-misconduct/story?id=51956410

xiii Jacobs, Ben, et al. "'You can do anything': Trump brags on tape about using fame to get women: Republicans line up to condemn presidential nominee as lewd bragging about using fame for sexual advances horrifies allies and opponents alike" The Guardian, 8 Oct 2016, https://www.theguardian.com/us-news/2016/oct/07/donald-trump-leaked-recording-women

xiv Borchers, Callum. "Kellyanne Conway's persecution complex" The Washington Post, 5 Jun 2017, https://www.washingtonpost.com/news/the-fix/wp/2017/06/05/kellyanne-conways-persecution-complex/

xv Beckel, Michael. "Super PACs Dominate 2016 Republican TV Ads So Far" Center for Public Integrity, Washington, D.C. Time.com, 16 Sep 2015, https://time.com/4036969/campaign-ads-super-pacs/

xvi Rupar, Aaron. "What's illegal about Trump's hush payments to women, briefly explained: Debunking the president's desperate spin about being incriminated in felonies." Vox, 12 Dec 2018, https://www.vox.com/2018/12/12/18138213/trump-illegal-hush-payments-women-explained

xvii Benko, Ralph. "Donald Trump, Political Mass Hypnotist?" Forbes, 28 Nov 2015, https://www.forbes.com/sites/ralphbenko/2015/11/28/donald-trump-political-mass-hypnotist/#3d0cf78852fd

xviii Aristotle. Rhetoric. Athens, Greece, 322 BCE.

xix Breuninger, Kevin. "Trump claimed he turned a 'small' $1 million loan from his father into an empire. The New York Times says it was more like $60.7 million in loans" CNBC.com, 2 Oct 2018, https://www.cnbc.com/2018/10/02/trumps-small-loan-from-his-father-was-more-like-60point7-million-nyt.html

[xx] Calmes, Jackie. "Donald Trump: Campaigns and Elections" UVA Miller Center. https://millercenter.org/president/trump/campaigns-and-elections accessed 09 Aug 2020

[xxi] Durkin, Erin, and Edelman, Adam. "Donald Trump enters 2016 presidential race with bizarre speech insulting Mexican immigrants, lambasting Obama" NY Daily News, 17 Jun 2015, https://www.nydailynews.com/news/politics/donald-trump-entering-2016-presidential-race-article-1.2259706

[xxii] Leighley, Jan, and Nagler, Jonathan. Who Votes Now? Demographics, Issues, Inequality, and Turnout in the United States. Princeton, New Jersey: Princeton University Press, 2013.

[xxiii] Garber, Megan. "The Attention Games: What Americans choose to concentrate on, now more than ever, is an ethical matter." The Atlantic, 2 Nov 2018, https://www.theatlantic.com/entertainment/archive/2018/11/donald-trump-and-ethics-attention/574741/

[xxiv] Buettner, Russ, and Craig, Susanne. "Decade in the Red: Trump Tax Figures Show over $1 Billion in Business Losses" The New York Times, 08 May 2019, https://www.nytimes.com/interactive/2019/05/07/us/politics/donald-trump-taxes.html

[xxv] Barrett, Mark. "'Hold your nose and vote,' Graham tells Christians" Citizen Times, 15 Oct 2016, https://www.citizen-times.com/story/news/politics/elections/2016/10/15/hold-your-nose-and-vote-graham-tells-christians/92139852/

[xxvi] Nordquist, Richard. "Definition and Examples of Evidence in Argument" thoughtco. 13 Feb 2019, https://www.thoughtco.com/evidence-argument-term-1690682

[xxvii] Beastie Boys. "So What'Cha Want." Check Your Head, Capitol, 1992. CD Single.

[xxviii] Corey, Amy. "Chapter I: Introducing Communication." The Evolution of Human Communication: From Theory to Practice, by Tess Pierce, Ontario, Ontario: eCampusOntario. https://ecampusontario.pressbooks.pub/evolutionhumancommunication/chapter/chapter-1/ accessed 09 Aug 2020

[xxix] Levine, Mike. "'No Blame?' ABC News finds 54 cases invoking 'Trump' in connection with violence, threats, alleged assaults. President Donald Trump insists he deserves no blame for divisions in America." abcnews, 30 May 2020, https://abcnews.go.com/Politics/blame-abc-news-finds-17-cases-invoking-trump/story?id=58912889

[xxx] Confessor, Nicholas, and Yourish, Karen. "$2 Billion Worth of Free Media for Donald Trump" The New York Times, 15 Mar 2016, https://www.nytimes.com/2016/03/16/upshot/measuring-donald-trumps-mammoth-advantage-in-free-media.html

[xxxi] Graves, Allison. "Trump says the media doesn't show his crowds at rallies. He's wrong" Politifact, 03 Nov 2016, https://www.politifact.com/factchecks/2016/nov/03/donald-trump/trump-says-media-doesnt-show-his-crowds-rallies-he/

[xxxii] Cobb, Jelani. "The Supreme Court Just Legitimized a Cornerstone Element of Voter Suppression" The New Yorker, 03 Jul 2019, https://www.newyorker.com/news/daily-comment/the-supreme-court-just-legitimized-a-cornerstone-element-of-voter-suppression

[xxxiii] "For Most Trump Voters, 'Very Warm' Feelings for Him Endured: Also: A detailed look at the 2016 electorate, based on voter records." Pew Research Center, Washington, D.C. 09 Aug 2018, https://www.pewresearch.org/politics/2018/08/09/for-most-trump-voters-very-warm-feelings-for-him-endured/

[xxxiv] Primoratz, Igor. "Patriotism", *The Stanford Encyclopedia of Philosophy* (Spring 2019 Edition), Edward N. Zalta (ed.), https://plato.stanford.edu/archives/spr2019/entries/patriotism

[xxxv] Felty, Stephan M. *Social Identity Theory and Intergroup Conflict in Israel/Palestine.* MA Thesis. Naval Postgraduate School, March 2019. https://www.hsdl.org/?view&did=825217 accessed 03 Aug 2020

[xxxvi] Robbins, Stephen, and Coulter, Mary. Management: Seventh Edition. Upper Saddle River, New Jersey: Prentice Hall, 2003.

xxxvii Solomon, David and Israel, Harold. "Fiduciary Duties of Boards of Directors of Financially Distressed Companies in the Time of COVID" Levenfeld Pearlstein, LLC, 18 Jun 2020, https://www.lplegal.com/content/fiduciary-duties-boards-of-directors-financially-distressed-companies.html

xxxviii Mueller, III, Robert. *Report On The Investigation Into Russian Interference In The 2016 Presidential Election*. Washington D.C.: US Department of Justice, 2019. PDF. Volume II. https://www.justice.gov/storage/report_volume2.pdf

xxxix Koontz, Harold, and O'Donnell. Principles of Management: An Analysis of Managerial Functions. New York City, New York. McGraw Hill Book Company, 1968.

xl Schwab, Nikki. "Donald Trump has built just THREE MILES of entirely new border wall where no barrier existed before, Department of Homeland Security reveals" DailyMail.com, 27 May 2020, https://www.dailymail.co.uk/news/article-8361947/Trump-built-just-THREE-MILES-entirely-new-border-wall.html

xli Todd, Chuck, et al. "All pain, no gain: Trump ends up with the same border deal he once rejected" Meet the Press, NBC News, 14 Feb 2019, https://www.nbcnews.com/politics/meet-the-press/all-pain-no-gain-trump-ends-same-border-deal-he-n971466

xlii Valverde, Miriam. "Here's what Donald Trump did his first week as president of the United States" Politifact, 27 Jan 2017, https://www.politifact.com/article/2017/jan/27/heres-what-donald-trump-did-first-week-president-u/

xliii Lalljee, Jason. "Trump weighing executive order to force insurers to cover pre-existing conditions, something Obamacare does" USA Today, 08 Aug 2020, https://www.usatoday.com/story/news/politics/2020/08/08/trump-pursuing-executive-order-covering-pre-existing-conditions/3326123001/

xliv Wamhoff, Steve. "How Much Will Typical Middle-Class Workers Really See Their Paychecks Change?" Institute on Taxation and Economic Policy, 03 Feb 2018, https://itep.org/how-much-will-typical-middle-class-workers-really-see-their-paychecks-change/

[xlv] Gajanan, Mahita. "Trump's Trade War With China Could Cost the Average Family Up to $2,300 a Year, Report Estimates" Time, 14 May 2019, https://time.com/5587197/trump-china-trade-war-cost-families/

[xlvi] Hass, Ryan. "Time to rethink U.S. trade strategy in Asia" Brookings, 20 Feb 2018, https://www.brookings.edu/blog/order-from-chaos/2018/02/20/time-to-rethink-u-s-trade-strategy-in-asia/

[xlvii] "Indo-Pacific Strategies of U.S. Allies and Partners: Issues for Congress" EveryCRSReport.com, 30 Jan 2020, https://www.everycrsreport.com/reports/R46217.html#_Toc31982425 accessed 12 Aug 2020

[xlviii] McLaughlin, Elizabeth, and Finnegan, Conor. "The truth about President Trump's $110 billion Saudi arms deal: ABC News found that only approximately $25 billion is in the actual pipeline." abcnews, 06 Jun 2017, https://abcnews.go.com/International/truth-president-trumps-110-billion-saudi-arms-deal/story?id=47874726

[xlix] Robiou, Marcia. "What You Need to Know About Trump's $8 Billion Saudi Arms Deal" PBS Frontline, 16 Jul 2019, https://www.pbs.org/wgbh/frontline/article/saudi-arabia-arms-deal-trump-what-to-know/

[l] Lemon, Jason. "Trump Defends Saudi Arabia's Murder of Journalist Jamal Khashoggi by Saying Iran Kills People Too" Newsweek, 23 Jun 2019, https://www.newsweek.com/trump-defends-saudi-arabia-jamal-khashoggi-iran-kills-people-1445430

[li] Farrell, Henry. "Trump's plan to work with Putin on cybersecurity makes no sense. Here's why." The Washington Post, 09 Jul 2017, https://www.washingtonpost.com/news/monkey-cage/wp/2017/07/09/trumps-plan-to-work-with-putin-on-cybersecurity-makes-no-sense-heres-why/

[lii] Beauchamp, Zack. "MOAB, the largest non-nuclear bomb ever used by the US military, explained" Vox, 14 Apr 2017, https://www.vox.com/world/2017/4/13/15292418/moab-mother-of-all-bombs

[liii] Bloom, Dan. "Donald Trump bragged about bombing Syria to Chinese President while eating 'the most beautiful chocolate cake': Donald Trump has told how President Xi was enjoying pudding in Florida when he authorised a missile strike on "Iraq" - no, wait, Syria" Mirror, 12 Apr 2017, https://www.mirror.co.uk/news/politics/donald-trump-bragged-bombing-syria-10212059

[liv] "Big Business: Steel and Oil" CliffsNotes.com. Houghton Mifflin Harcourt., 2020. https://www.cliffsnotes.com/study-guides/history/us-history-ii/industrial-america/big-business-steel-and-oil accessed 08 Aug 2020.

[lv] "Economic Concepts for Understanding Media" Burlington, Vermont: UVM. http://www.uvm.edu/~tstreete/Courses/Soc43/pages/lecture_economicconcepts.html accessed 08 Aug 2020.

[lvi] Kapur, Sahil, and Dennis, Steven. How Trump Let His Goal of Building a Border Wall Slip Away" Bloomberg, 13 Dec 2018, https://www.bloomberg.com/news/articles/2018-12-13/how-trump-let-his-goal-of-building-a-border-wall-slip-away

[lvii] Jacobson, Louis. "Has the Trump administration spent only 6 percent of border money?" Politifact, 4 Jan 2019, https://www.politifact.com/factchecks/2019/jan/04/chris-murphy/has-trump-administration-spent-only-6-percent-bord/

[lviii] Rennie, Jon. "Are Employees an Expense or an Asset? The Answer May Surprise You (Resource Management)" LeadX, 19 Oct 2017, https://leadx.org/articles/employees-expense-asset-answer-may-surprise/

[lix] Friedman, Uri. "Inside the Collapse of Trump's Korea Policy: When it comes to America's last-ditch effort to prevent North Korea from becoming a nuclear power, timing has been everything. Now time's running out." The Atlantic, 19 Dec 2019, https://www.theatlantic.com/politics/archive/2019/12/donald-trump-kim-jong-un-north-korea-diplomacy-denuclearization/603748/

[lx] Tuccille, J.D. "Bill Barr Knew He Would Be a Hatchet Man for Trump: Barr's big complaint is that the president is so overt with the sleazy pressure." reason, 18 Feb 2020, https://reason.com/2020/02/18/bill-barr-knew-he-would-be-a-hatchet-man-for-trump/

lxi Hollis-Brusky, Amanda. "What Is The Federalist Society And How Does It Affect Supreme Court Picks?" *All Things Considered*. NPR.org, 28 Jun 2018, https://www.npr.org/2018/06/28/624416666/what-is-the-federalist-society-and-how-does-it-affect-supreme-court-picks

lxii Zurcher, Anthony. "Why doesn't Trump fire people to their face?" BBC News, 15 Mar 2018, https://www.bbc.com/news/world-us-canada-43421000

lxiii Chait, Jonathan. "Trump Fires Defense Official for Refusing to Break the Law on His Behalf" *New York*, 11 Feb 2020, https://nymag.com/intelligencer/2020/02/trump-fires-defense-official-refusing-to-break-law-elaine-mccusker.html

lxiv Manktelow, James, and Birkinshaw, Julian. "One of the hallmarks of a truly great boss has nothing to do with vision or work ethic" Business Insider, 21 May 2018, https://www.businessinsider.com/emotional-intelligence-tact-make-great-bosses-2018-5

lxv Trump, Donald. "Meet the Billionaire" *The Apprentice*. NBC, 8 Jan 2004. Television.

lxvi Shapiro, Ariel. "White House Coronavirus Briefing Back On After Cancellation This Morning" Forbes, 27 Apr 2020, https://www.forbes.com/sites/arielshapiro/2020/04/27/white-house-coronavirus-briefing-back-on-after-cancellation-this-morning/#44ba3b357d68

lxvii Dawsey, Josh, and McGinley, Laurie. "Trump backs off flavored vape ban he once touted" Washington Post, 17 Nov 2019, https://www.washingtonpost.com/national/health-science/trump-pulls-back-from-flavored-vaping-ban/2019/11/17/30853ece-07ae-11ea-924a-28d87132c7ec_story.html

lxviii Waldman, Simon. "Trump Is Complicit in Erdogan's Ethnic Cleansing: What Turkey's president is openly planning is the forced exchange of one ethnic population for another. That's Ethnic Cleansing 101. And Trump rolled over to let it happen" Haaretz, 10 Oct 2019, https://www.haaretz.com/middle-east-news/.premium-trump-is-complicit-in-erdogan-s-ethnic-cleansing-of-the-kurds-in-syria-1.7963502

lxix *Airplane!* Directed by Jim Abrahams, et al., performance by Leslie Nielsen, Paramount Pictures, 1980.

lxx Brookins, Miranda. "What Is the Purpose of Internal Controls of a Company?" Chron, 04 Feb 2019, https://smallbusiness.chron.com/purpose-internal-controls-company-12116.html

lxxi "management control" BusinessDictionary, WebFinance Inc, 2020, http://www.businessdictionary.com/definition/management-control.html

lxxii United States. Senate. Select Committee on Intelligence. *Russian Active Measures Campaigns and Interference in the 2016 U.S. Election Volume 1: Russian Efforts Against Election Infrastructure with Additional Views.* Washington D.C., 2020, https://www.intelligence.senate.gov/sites/default/files/documents/Report_Volume1.pdf

lxxiii Geller, Eric. "Trump-Putin meeting rekindles ridiculed cyber plan" Politico, 16 Jul 2018, https://www.politico.com/story/2018/07/16/trump-putin-russia-cybersecurity-689470

lxxiv Embury-Dennis, Tom. "Trump refuses to impose new Russia sanctions despite law passed by US Congress over election hacking: 'It just doesn't make sense'" Independent, 20 Jan 2018, https://www.independent.co.uk/news/world/americas/us-russia-sanctions-trump-no-new-congress-law-election-hacking-intervention-putin-kremlin-a8184866.html

lxxv Gardner, Lauren. "Forget Mexico: Democrats turn focus to porous Canadian border: While the White House is asking for more money and manpower at the southern border, staffing at the U.S.-Canada boundary is floundering." Politico, 13 Jan 2019, https://www.politico.com/story/2019/01/11/congress-canada-mexico-border-security-terrorism-1071243

lxxvi Schwartz, Jeremy, and Trevizo, Perla. "He Built a Privately Funded Border Wall. It's Already at Risk of Falling Down if Not Fixed. Trump supporters funded a private border wall on the banks of the Rio Grande, helping the builder secure $1.7 billion in federal contracts. Now the "Lamborghini" of border walls is in danger of falling into the river if nothing is done, experts say." Propublica, 02 Jul 2020, https://www.propublica.org/article/he-built-a-privately-funded-border-wall-its-already-at-risk-of-falling-down-if-not-fixed [lxxvii] Berman, Russell. "How Democrats Stopped Worrying and Learned to Accept Trump's Wall: Senator Chuck Schumer's offer to fund the border wall as part of a deal on DACA did not come out of the blue: It reflects a shift in Democratic priorities on immigration that has been months in the making." The Atlantic, 24 Jan 2018, https://www.theatlantic.com/politics/archive/2018/01/democrats-schumer-trump-border-wall-daca/551288/

[lxxviii] Holland, Steve, and Cowan, Richard. "Backing down, Trump agrees to end shutdown without border wall money" Reuters, 25, Jan 2019 , https://www.reuters.com/article/us-usa-shutdown/backing-down-trump-agrees-to-end-shutdown-without-border-wall-money-idUSKCN1PJ126

[lxxix] Stein, Benjamin, and Stein, Herbert. Moneypower: How to Make Inflation Make You Rich. New York, New York: Harper & Row, 1979.

[lxxx] Buettner, Russ, and Craig, Susanne. "Decade in the Red: Trump Tax Figures" New York Times, 08 May 2019, https://www.nytimes.com/interactive/2019/05/07/us/politics/donald-trump-taxes.html

[lxxxi] Newman, Rick. "Why Trump wants to manipulate the Federal Reserve" Yahoo Finance, 09 Apr 2019, https://finance.yahoo.com/news/why-trump-wants-to-manipulate-the-federal-reserve-123602758.html

[lxxxii] Cox, Jeff. "Trump says he has the right to remove Powell as Fed chair but hasn't 'made any decisions' yet" CNBC, 14 Mar 2020, https://www.cnbc.com/2020/03/14/trump-says-he-has-the-right-to-remove-powell-as-fed-chair-but-hasnt-made-any-decisions-yet.html

[lxxxiii] "Trump's Fed pick Stephen Moore withdraws name after losing Republican support: Moore had also come under fire for his writings about women." Associated Press, 02 May 2019, https://www.pressherald.com/2019/05/02/trumps-fed-pick-stephen-moore-withdraws-name-amid-loss-of-gop-support-controversy-over-writings-about-women/

lxxxiv Clark, Dartunorro. "Trump suggests 'injection' of disinfectant to beat coronavirus and 'clean' the lungs: A Homeland Security official, under questioning from reporters, later said federal laboratories are not considering such a treatment option." NBC New, 23 Apr 2020, https://www.nbcnews.com/politics/donald-trump/trump-suggests-injection-disinfectant-beat-coronavirus-clean-lungs-n1191216

lxxxv Gibson, Carl. "Workers Are Getting the Short End of the Stick from the Cares Act" Barron's, 15 Apr 2020, https://www.barrons.com/articles/cares-act-workers-companies-unfair-coronavirus-aid-51586983332

lxxxvi Carey, Henry. Principles of Social Science. Philadelphia, Pennsylvania, London, England: J. B. Lippincott & co., Trübner & co.; [etc., etc.], 1858-59.

lxxxvii Horsley, Scott. "After 2 Years, Trump Tax Cuts Have Failed To Deliver On GOP's Promises" npr.org, 20 Dec 2019, https://www.npr.org/2019/12/20/789540931/2-years-later-trump-tax-cuts-have-failed-to-deliver-on-gops-promises

lxxxviii Gleckman, Howard, and Boddupalli, Aravind. "The US Economy Reverts To A Pre-Tax Cut Growth Rate" Tax Policy Center, 01 Aug 2019, https://www.taxpolicycenter.org/taxvox/us-economy-reverts-pre-tax-cut-growth-rate

lxxxix Jahan, Sarwat, et al. "What Is Keynesian Economics?" Finance & Development, Sep 2014, https://www.imf.org/external/pubs/ft/fandd/2014/09/basics.htm accessed 17 Aug 2020.

xc Chait, Jonathan. "Trump Cites Sole Triumph: Rebranding Obama's Economy As His Own" New York, 04 Feb 2020, https://nymag.com/intelligencer/2020/02/trump-cites-sole-triumph-rebranding-obamas-economy-as-his.html

xci United States. Department of Energy. Energy Information Administration. "Despite the U.S. becoming a net petroleum exporter, most regions are still net importers" Today in Energy, 06 Feb 2020, https://www.eia.gov/todayinenergy/detail.php?id=42735

xcii Rand, Ayn. Atlas Shrugged. New York, New York: Signet, 1996.